This book is a gift to

_____

Date

_____

From

_____

This book is dedicated to my own dad,
Douglas R. Moore, who is a powerful example
of steadfast love in every circumstance.
Thanks, Dad, for being you.
Love, Karen

For you, Dad

... because I love you.

Karen Moore

christian
art gifts ®

For you, Dad

Introduction

Dad, this book is for you because you are an incredible father and an amazing person. You're a loving example to your children, your family, and your friends.

There's no one quite like you and it's easy to see God's fingerprints on your life. Thank you for being such a wonderful dad! May God bless you abundantly.

Karen Moore

MADE IN GOD'S IMAGE

Most children grow up looking for ways they can imitate their moms and dads. After all, moms and dads are the best role models; the ones who help them to see how to fit into the world.

As parents, we're usually happy when we see the very best aspects of ourselves reflected in the young faces of our offspring. In fact, we often take pride in the very things kids do that are just like us.

You set an example of what it means to follow in God's footsteps and to be as much like Him as you can. That desire on your part comes through in all you do. As you reflect God's image, others see what it really means to have a loving relationship with the Creator of the heavens and the earth. You mirror His goodness in very special ways.

You're probably thinking that you don't remember doing all those wonderful things, but that's just the point. You do them so naturally, it feels effortless. You take the idea of putting on the image and the armor of God so personally that the result is found in more peace, more joy, and more contentment for all those who connect with you.

Your peaceful assurance comes from the confident grace that allows God's image to shine through you.

As parents smile on their children for doing the best they can in any situation, your Father smiles on you for the same reason.

Today, you're being recognized for the genuine love and generous spirit that you have toward everyone you encounter.

Thanks for being such a light and thanks for doing your best to reflect the love of the One who made you. There's nobody quite like you and it's easy to see God's fingerprints on your life.

Lord, may Your blessing rest
forever on the head and shoulders
of this amazing dad as he works to be
the special person You created him
to be for You and for his family.
Amen.

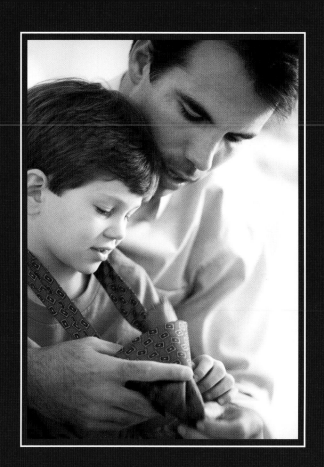

One father is more than
a hundred schoolmasters.

- George Herbert -

From Fathers to Dads

Fathers were once considered the law-givers of the household and rarely interacted with their children apart from offering disciplinary measures. Over time, fathers became sought after for their wise advice and direction. Today's fathers are either very involved or modestly involved or simply absent from their children's lives.

When Sonora Smart Dodd initiated the idea of Father's Day, it was because she was so proud of her own father who was a civil war veteran and single-handedly raised six children. Calvin Coolidge got the ball rolling to create a national public holiday for fathers, but it wasn't made an official holiday until the time of Richard Nixon. Greeting cards and backyard barbecues aside, fathers deserve to be celebrated, especially fathers like you!

Mothers may well be the heart of most homes, but fathers shape, guide and offer the balance that helps a child understand more fully what our Creator God is like. William Wordsworth said this about the word, *father*: "Father! – To God Himself we cannot give a holier name!"

Good fathers, like you, are those who shine a light on what God wants for His children. You help your children to discover God's love because you share your heart and your kindness with them each day. You have taken the role of father very seriously and made it even more special. It's been said that "anyone can be a father, but it takes someone special to be a dad."

You're a dad who is kind, loving, and generous towards your children. You deserve to be celebrated for all you do to make life better for those in your care.

It is easier for a father to have children
than it is for children to have a real father.
~ Pope John XXIII ~

And you, fathers,
do not provoke your children
to wrath, but bring them
up in the training and
admonition of the Lord.

- Ephesians 6:4 NKJV -

Lord, thank You for the kind and
loving hearts of fathers who strive
every day to be even better dads.
Amen.

THE ESSENTIALS OF LIFE

Water, food, and oxygen are not the only ingredients that are necessary to sustain life. Though all of these are necessary to the body, the spirit has cravings of its own. The spirit needs hope, love, and encouragement. Good fathers like you recognize how important those needs are and attend to them with just as much fervor and energy as they do to support the family's financial resources.

You offer hope each time you help your children to recognize other options, other roads that can be traveled, richer opportunities for dreams to come true. You offer hope for the future for better things to come, just as God did for all of His children through the words in Jeremiah 29:11, "I know the plans I have for you," declares the Lord, "plans to prosper you and not to harm you, plans to give you hope and a future" (NIV). You are a father who helps sustain the future with a possibility of infinite hope and of greater things yet to come.

Without question, you offer love in every way you can to enrich your children's lives. Because of your love, they can understand the love of their heavenly Father in a much fuller way. They can see Him and understand 1 John 4:19, "We love because

He first loved us" (NIV). You're an example of that kind of love in thought, word, and deed. How blessed your children are!

And finally, you understand that to be human is to live with times of disappointment and wonder. Your children have the example you offer of trusting in a brighter tomorrow and moving forward with confidence that prayers are answered and new paths are opened.

You encourage your children's belief in the goodness of life and all that God meant for them to have. You're a father who continually enriches their growth and their well being because you understand these things so well.

> The next best thing to being wise oneself is to live in a circle of those who are.
>
> ~ C. S. Lewis ~

Lord, please bless Your son
and the work he does as a father.
Grant him wisdom and insight
to understand the needs and
fears and dreams of his children
in such a way that they may
all be truly blessed.
Amen.

*"I have come that they may have life,
and that they may have it more abundantly."*

- John 10:10 NKJV -

FATHERS AND THE GAME OF LIFE

Fathers are the ones who give their children the best pieces on the game board of life so they can play well. With the right understanding of the game, a child learns that one path is better than another. One move may set you back a bit, but another one sends you on ahead a little faster than even you thought you would go.

Fathers like you do this by letting children know what the rules are right from the start. You know how the game is played and you know the consequences off the course too. You set the opportunity for your children to get to the winners' circle. You do that every day because you're such an incredible dad.

In our culture, games are taken seriously. Whether we're watching team sports, tennis matches or chess championships, the rules of the game are watched closely. To trespass those rules can mean losing the game. This kind of thinking has been going on for centuries with a variety of players.

Michel de Montaigne quoted Pythagoras as he observed the Olympic Games. Pythagoras said, "A few men strain their muscles to carry off the prize; others bring trinkets to sell to the crowd for gain; and some there are, and not the worst, who seek no other profit than to look at the show and see how and why everything is done; spectators of the life of other men in order to judge and regulate their own."

As a dad, you've helped your children get in the game, playing with the best skills they have. You've shown them that sitting on the sidelines might not be a problem for some games, but that sitting and judging others will only cause you to stay further away from joining the game yourself.

Thanks for teaching your children to learn the rules, play fair, and take a chance when the game is on so that they can move forward and make a difference in the world.

You're a great coach, Dad!

Heavenly Father, thank You
for the kind of dad who helps his
children not only to understand the rules,
but to play the game of life by these rules.
Thanks for the dads who help their
children become winners in every way.
Amen.

Winners look for answers

with a *positive* result,

losers look for problems

and a place to put the fault.

Winners make *decisions*

when they have a chance to choose,

losers make excuses

when it looks like they might lose.

Winners say, "I'll do it,

whatever must be done,"

Losers say, "Don't look at me,

I've simply got to run."

TIPS FOR A SUCCESSFUL LIFE

Dads are good at sharing bits of wisdom they've gleaned along the way so their children can avoid some of the more difficult moments they've already lived through. They recognize that nobody grows up without making mistakes and doing foolish things, so they do their best to guide their offspring into wise choices.

If you're thinking that sounds good, but you can't remember the last time your kids actually listened to you, then it's time to give yourself a little pat on the back for all the efforts you've made. You also need to think back to when you were in their shoes, and it won't take long to realize that in truth, more of what your parents taught you got through than you ever cared to admit back then. The same is true for your own children. They may not readily acknowledge your little proverbs, but they hear them just the same.

What kinds of things do you share with them? Sometimes you want them to understand that life isn't always easy and that people are not always considerate or kind. In fact, some people cause you to learn patience and tolerance beyond what you ever hoped to learn. As a good dad, you speak to that situation with love.

You teach them that hardships happen to everyone. Unexpected things can fall like rain on a clear blue day, long before you can find an umbrella. You teach them how to make the best of the clouds they encounter and how to wait with patience and trust for the sun to come out again. You influence their thoughts toward positive change.

You teach your children to appreciate what they have because you let them know so readily what they mean to you and what your home means to you. They get to see first hand that good things need to be cherished and that God needs to be thanked for those things on a regular basis.

You're a good teacher, giving your children a wealth of great tips to make it through life. You guide them well and everyone around you is grateful for your leadership and love.

Dear God, please bless the man who teaches his children to observe the world around them, to give thanks for what they have, and to appreciate all that You have done to bring grace and abundance to life.

Amen.

"Seek first God's kingdom and what God wants. Then all your other needs will be met as well. So don't worry about tomorrow, because tomorrow will have its own worries."

- Matthew 6:33-34 -

Life is a hard fight, a struggle, a wrestling with the principle of evil, hand to hand, foot to foot. Every inch of the way is disputed. The night is given us to take breath, to pray, to drink deep at the fountain of power; the day to use the strength which has been given us, to go forth to work with it till the evening.

- Florence Nightingale -

You're a Generous Dad

Generous is such a positive word! If we apply it to our Father in heaven then we can easily understand the meaning. After all, we just have to start counting our blessings, and if our counting took in everything we have, it would show us God has been very generous.

A dad like you has that same generous spirit, that same open heart and open hand that draws others to you. You're an example of just how BIG love and generosity can be.

You have taught your children to be generous too. You show them that part of generosity is simply about giving your heart and letting it overflow with joy. You do that by offering to help others, embracing your family, and giving the best of yourself in every circumstance. You help everyone to see the benefits of lavishing good things on those around you.

An ancient Persian proverb says this about generosity: "What I kept, I lost, what I spent, I had, what I gave, I have." The only thing that we keep then are those things that we give away with a generous heart and spirit just as our loving Father gives to us.

Frederick Buechner said, "The world says, the more you take, the more you have. Christ says, the more you give, the more you are." Dad, thank you for teaching your family this secret.

Thank you for being a generous giver, a loving dad and a faithful friend. Thank you for being an example that will live on in your children. Thank you for teaching your children that a generous and open heart helps God's Spirit pour abundant grace and love on all who come near.

Dear Father, please bless the gifts
of this generous and loving man.
Bless his heart and mind and spirit
in ways that nourish him so that
he may continue to be all that
You mean for him to be, to share,
and to give to those around him.
Amen.

Giving is the secret of a healthy life.

Not necessarily money,

but whatever a man has of encouragement

and sympathy and understanding.

- John D. Rockefeller, Jr. -

Remember this: The person who plants a little will have a small harvest, but the person who plants a lot will have a big harvest. Each of you should give as you have decided in your heart to give.

- 2 Corinthians 9:6-7 -

Giving and Giving In

Most fathers enjoy giving all they can to their families. It's a natural part of what makes them thrive and have happy hearts. Sometimes the experience of being a giving dad can mean making the choices about when it's good to be giving and when you might find yourself in a state of compromise, perhaps "giving in" when it doesn't feel like the wisest course. What happens then? What can you do, Dad, when you feel like you gave in to something that didn't quite sit with you the way you wanted?

As we look at that kind of situation, we might wonder whether God ever does that with us. Does our Father in heaven, ready to give us what we need for our greater good, ever simply "give in" to our wishes, fully knowing there's a risk involved, because He so respects who we are? That's the choice a good parent makes all the time, and you're the kind of dad who carefully looks at that experience and wisely gives in when the issue at hand calls for you to do so.

Giving in at the right time can actually be the right kind of giving. Giving in generally means you didn't quite agree, but you believe your child has a right to learn and grow from the choices being made. You give in to life's opportunity and God's grace and protection to watch over your child, even when you feel slightly uneasy about it. Giving in isn't the same as giving up, it's recognizing how important it is for each person, each child of God to come to terms with what life offers and discover the best path to follow.

As a dad, you've chosen to give in to letting your child grow, discover, change and even fail. You've chosen to give in to what your child wants, even if you believe it is not the best course, knowing that you're helping your child grow and learn.

You've also chosen to give in to the will of God in a sacred moment and rest your fears and anxieties in His hand. You've been a wise giver and you've given in wisely too, knowing God's fingerprint is on each of His children and He is wholly involved in their parenting.

"We are allowed to do all things,"
but not all things are good for us to do.
"We are allowed to do all things,"
but not all things help others grow stronger.
Do not look out only for yourselves.
Look out for the good of others also.

- 1 Corinthians 10:23-24 -

Lord, thank You for walking with Your sons who are making an effort to be wise and loving parents. Help them to know that when they have a sense that it's time for them to give in, then it's just the start of when You can give even more to the situation at hand. Bless each giving dad.

Amen.

THE GIFT OF FRIENDSHIP STARTS AT HOME

Sometimes fathers don't recognize that they can actually be strong parents and still cultivate a spirit of friendship with their children. It may be a popular notion that at certain times in a child's life they have a need for your authority more than your friendship, but the truth is, they always need to know your love and respect as a person. Accepting your authority and being willing to be guided by you comes from knowing how good and wise you are.

The best dads respect their children and their children respect them right back. It comes from achieving a balance of what we might think of as authority over what we recognize as fairness and honoring each other's needs.

You achieve that balance. You offer a healthy mix of friendship and fatherliness so that your family can live in harmony and your children know it's safe to ask your opinion and seek your guidance. The blessing of your parenting skills shows in every positive way. When your children displease you, it's an event for you and for them. Neither party wants a measure of displeasure to enter the relationship. Why? Because you have worked through the years to communicate and help each other understand how you perceive life and what complicates things for you. You have built a foundation of trust both as parent and friend.

This gift that you've employed in raising your children may have started in your home, but it will move into every area of your child's life experience. It will be the cornerstone of how they operate in the world, what they expect from others and what they do to negotiate skillfully through life's ups and downs.

This gift of balance between fatherhood and friendship is one that makes those around you want to stand up and cheer. It is for this reason, and many others as well, that you have healthy and happy children who respect you, love life, and honor their Father in heaven.

Lord, help all dads to recognize
that there is a healthy balance between
wisdom and authority, and it stems
from a gracious and generous spirit.
Bless fathers who offer their children
both firm footing and friendship
as they go their way.
Amen.

The father of a good child is very happy; parents who
have wise children are glad because of them.

- Proverbs 23:24 -

Neighborly Dads

It's always fun to picture Dad as the king of the grill, the master of the backyard barbecue and a friend to all those who live nearby. It's a picture that we hold dear because in many ways, we recognize the deeper significance it brings when Dad is not only good to his family, but good to his neighbors too.

The dad who generously cares for the neighbor's yard when they are on a vacation, or lends a hand when the new garage is being built, is one that brings honor and blessing to everyone.

We live in a world that seems to applaud the workaholic dads who never have time to flip a burger or notice the grass growing in a neighbor's yard. The dads who do set limits and recognize that quality of life has everything to do with being a good neighbor rather than an absent father, can make a difference. Thanks for being the kind of dad who really strives for that balance. You know how to honor your work space, family space and that of your neighbors so that harmony can be achieved. It's not easy, but you do it and you deserve special recognition for the enormous effort you make.

If it isn't enough that you can see the smiles on the faces of members of your own family, then it's even more joyful to recognize that you can step outside and hear someone nearby call your name. They may not need your help, but they need your friendship and they love to connect with your generous spirit. You have a way of bringing Christ to your neighborhood and you do it by offering the bread of joy with an ample serving of grilled salmon to feast upon.

You have a way of making a difference that brings honor to your home and fills your family with pride. Your children are comfortable bringing their friends home because they have you, a dad who will offer his kind heart and generous spirit to each one who enters the door.

The *love of God* is the first

and greatest commandment.

But love of our neighbor

is the means by which we obey it.

Since we cannot see God directly,

God allows us to catch sight of

Him through our neighbor.

By *loving our neighbor* we purge

our eyes to see God.

So love your neighbor and you

will discover that in doing so

you come to know *God*.

- St. Augustine -

Lord, bless the dads who are good neighbors. Bless them as they offer to lend a helping hand, lift a saddened spirit, or cook a gracious meal. Dads are Your representatives on this earth and we thank You for each one of them.

Amen.

❧

"If your neighbor does something wrong, tell him about it, or you will be partly to blame. Forget about the wrong things people do to you, and do not try to get even. Love your neighbor as you love yourself."

- Leviticus 19:17-18 -

Dad Goes to Church

It's apparent that God looks to men for leadership when it comes to matters of faith. He carved them out as disciples, hand-picking those who would follow Him. He left the church in the hands of one of them with the full intention that the church would grow and men and women everywhere would come to respect and love being part of it.

He did all of that, and yet, in our day, few men take that role very seriously. Few see themselves as leaders in the church, or beyond that, spiritual heads of their homes.

What we've seen then is women who have stepped up to fill that space because the work needs to be accomplished and God honors the work of all His leaders, both male and female. All of this is meant to acknowledge you as a very special dad because you do lead and you do honor God in church and at home. You have answered the call that God extends to all of us with enthusiasm and love.

E. M. Bounds once commented, "What the church needs today is not more or better machinery, not new organizations, or more novel methods; but men whom the Holy

Spirit can use – men of prayer, men mighty in prayer." Men who are mighty in prayer change the world. They change the church world, the neighborhood, and the home. They are the leaders God intended them to be.

What would our world be like if more men answered this call? What if more dads found time in their busy schedules to build up the church, and in turn, build up their families, giving them strength and power. Dads who go to church offer more to their children than dads who work or sleep in every Sunday. Dads who listen to their own heavenly Father simply have more to offer because they have a firm foundation.

Thanks for being a dad who stands on the living foundation of God's Word and listens for His voice through constant and tender prayer.

Christians in community must again
show the world, not merely family values,
but the bond of the love of Christ.

- Edmund Clowney -

Through *Christians* like

yourselves gathered in churches,

this extraordinary plan of *God*

is becoming known and talked

about even among the angels!

All this is proceeding along lines

planned all along by God and then

executed in Christ Jesus. When

we *trust in Him*, we're free to say

whatever needs to be said,

bold to go wherever we need to go.

- Ephesians 3:10-12 THE MESSAGE -

Lord, bless Dad as he goes to church.

Bless him as he seeks more of You,

more wisdom, strength and guidance.

Empower him to be all that he can be

for the greater good of his children

and for the cause of Christ.

Amen.

DADS HONOR AND REFLECT THEIR FATHER

It's become almost "old fashioned" in today's world to talk about giving honor to someone. Those of us who grew up with the notion that we should honor our parents because it was a commandment given to us hundreds of years ago, have a vague intellectual connection to the word. Still, we aren't really sure what it means.

To honor anyone has a lot to do with respecting them and holding them in high esteem. It means we look up to them. As a dad, you've always been good at giving honor to those around you and especially to your heavenly Father.

You are comfortable for everyone to know very clearly that you revere and respect your Creator. That's an incredible attitude to hold because it's not prevalent in this world's culture. It is one of the things that separates you from so many others.

Beyond your willingness and desire to show your respect for God, you do something else that's very important to those around you. You "reflect" your heavenly Father as well. You extend kindness, mercy and loyalty to your family and friends. You're fair-minded and reasonable, seldom jumping to conclusions without knowing all the facts. You value others above yourself and your example is one others should follow. You're a man after God's own heart.

Alexandre Dumas once stated, "Without respect, love cannot go far or rise high: it is an angel with but one wing."

You have been a dad who shows great respect for others, especially your children and so your love helps them grow and gives them wings.

Show respect for all people:
Love the brothers and sisters of God's
family, respect God, honor the king.

- 1 Peter 2:17 -

Dear heavenly Father, thank You for the dads that know You in a way that strengthens their love for their children. Thank You for giving them a glimpse of Your greatness, Your grace and Your mercy. May they continue to honor You all the days of their lives.

Amen.

The fear of the *Lord* is the
beginning of wisdom.
Happy the soul that has been awed
by a view of *God's* majesty,
that has had a vision of
God's awful greatness,
His ineffable holiness,
His perfect righteousness,
His irresistible *power*,
His sovereign grace.

– *Anonymous* –

YOU'RE A DAD WHO CAN STRETCH AND BEND

Stretching and bending can be formidable exercises for some dads, but you seem to have an elastic spirit that's willing to twist and turn at a moment's notice. You have learned that being flexible is a pretty important part of being a parent and it makes a difference in the lives of everyone around you.

Some dads really want the world to be black and white, being able to blow the whistle and pull out the rule book whenever something out of line happens.

The problem is that there really aren't too many situations that actually fit a rule book. That's why God tried to make it easier for His children. He gave us two very definite rules and everything else seems to simply be an expanded version of that theme.

His rules almost seem simple and yet to actually live by them turns out to be tricky, causing us to have to do deep knee bends in prayer and stretch our arms to heaven to seek His counsel.

His first rule is simply to love Him with all our hearts and souls and minds. Most days, you probably find that a reasonable request. You're the kind of dad who recognizes how important it is to keep this very rule in the front of your mind at all times.

His other rule though, the one that causes you to have to reach up a little further, endure a little more and grow a little stronger, is the one about loving others as yourself. Loving others may even seem like a reasonable thing to do, but there are times as a parent that it can become a bit tricky to stay focused on that rule. You do though.

You do because you know how important it is. You know that sometimes you have to work just as hard at the second part of that condition, which is all about loving yourself.

Some of the sadness we witness in the world comes from those who simply never quite understood these two simple rules.

Thank you for exercising your faith, your heart, and your love in ways that help everyone around you to stretch and grow as well.

Grow in the grace and knowledge
of our Lord and Savior Jesus Christ.

- 2 Peter 3:18 NIV -

❧⚜☙

Out of our beliefs are born deeds;
out of our deeds we form habits;
out of our habits grows our character;
and on our character we build our destiny.

- Henry Hancock -

$\mathcal{L}ord$, bless this dad for learning to place his love and his trust in You so that he can stretch and bend and not break as he parents his own children. Thank You for giving him a glimpse of heavenly parenting so he can use Your techniques with the children You've given him. Help him to guard and protect them and help strengthen them as they grow. Bless this wonderful dad, every day of his life!

$\mathcal{A}men$.

The Dad
Who Broke the Mold

In some ways, the culture we live in tries hard to mold us so that we perform like everybody else, think like everybody else, and manage our lives and our children in ways that others deem acceptable. That can be a good thing, or it can mean that we've stepped away from actually thinking for ourselves.

You're the kind of dad who breaks the mold, taking the road less traveled and offering more than the stereotyped image we've culturally created. Thank you for being an innovative and loving father.

How do you do that? First of all, it appears that you don't have a great desire to raise your children so that they become mirror images of you. That's a pretty amazing way to think all by itself. You raise your children to be themselves and to be the best that they can be, using the time tested values that you've taught them.

Teaching children to value others, to be honest in the things they do and to respect their elders, isn't raising them to look like you; it's raising them to be in the image of their Creator Father. That's what makes you such a remarkable dad. You look to your heavenly Father for guidance and then

offer what you've learned, your successes and failures, to your children so they can keep growing and learning themselves.

That's a pretty awesome perspective and one that sets you apart from the dads who don't quite understand God's incredible plan for each child's life.

Antoine de Saint-Exupery once said, "Each man must look to himself to teach him the meaning of life. It is not something discovered: it is something molded." You seem to have taken that principle, but developed it with the strength and love that comes from knowing Christ as your Savior. You have brought the best of these gifts to your family and especially to your children.

Thanks, Dad, for sharing your special and unique gifts with all those around you!

Life's Tug of War

Take the life that you have and give it your best,

be positive, *be happy*, let God do the rest,

take the challenges that life has laid at your feet,

take pride and be thankful for each one you meet.

To yourself give *forgiveness* if you stumble and fall,

take each day that is dealt you and give it your all,

take the love that you're given and return it with care,

have faith that when needed it will always be there.

Take time to find the beauty in the things that you see,

take life's simple *pleasures*; let them set your heart free,

the idea here is simply to even the score,

as you are met and faced with life's tug of war.

– *Anonymous* –

Lord God, thank You for the amazing dads who reflect Your heart to their children. Thank You for designing them so uniquely that they break the mold of the stereotypes of culture and become the kind of earthly fathers that help their children to see You! *Amen.*

Dad's Apology

Saying "I'm sorry" is a difficult thing for most of us. It's one of those things where we hope the other person will either forgive first or simply forget anything we may have done to offend them.

It's funny because sometimes we don't even know we need to apologize for one of those behaviors – we just assume others have to understand. When we don't have time to spend with our children, or we give them a look that says, "I'm not here for you right now" or "I'm not really interested in what you have to say," we might just console ourselves that it's okay, because it's just life.

But is it? The good news is that you're the kind of dad who does not take his children for granted. You know enough about yourself and you trust and respect your children enough that when a circumstance occurs that requires an apology, you give it.

That's not to say you don't hesitate a bit before it happens – feeling the grief of the situation is just natural, but you know that a lack of forgiveness on your part or your child's part not only affects the present, but very likely affects the future. It is, after all, the very reason Jesus died for us, so we could each be forgiven and have a future with our Father in heaven.

Thanks for being a father who is willing to express a desire for reconciliation whether the situation was actually your fault or not, but most notably when it was. As Samuel Johnson said, "A wise man will make haste to forgive, because he knows the true value of time, and will not suffer it to pass away in unnecessary pain." The hurt, discomfort and alienation of hiding from a need to talk about forgiveness, is beyond measure. It can last for generations in families that refuse to let go of the pain.

Thank you for being there and for being willing to let go. Thank you for bringing your children back to an understanding of what it truly means to live in grace. You are an example every day of God's love.

Father, thank You for teaching us how to forgive ourselves, our children, and even those random acts of the world that seem so out of our control. Help all fathers to be more loving and forgiving to the ones they cherish the most in life. *Amen.*

Dear Lord and Father of mankind,
Forgive our foolish ways!
Reclothe us in our rightful mind,
In purer lives Thy service find,
In deeper reverence, praise.

- John Greenleaf Whittier -

God has chosen you and made you
His holy people. *He loves you.*
So you should always clothe yourselves
with mercy, kindness, humility,
gentleness, and patience. Bear with
each other, and *forgive each other.*
If someone does wrong to you, forgive
that person because the Lord forgave
you. Even more than all this, clothe
yourself in love. Love is what holds
you all together in perfect unity.

- Colossians 3:12-14 -

Dad Never Gives Up!

Striving for anything that you hope will reflect well on you after you've achieved it, is hard work. While you're growing up, you strive to become the unique person you are and try to please your parents and those you trust and believe in. When you strike out on your own, you know the fears you have to overcome to make it in a world that isn't always forgiving, and is seldom easy. When you become a father you have a whole new reason for persistence, a whole new purpose in life. Now you have the job that requires more attention than anything else you've ever done.

You know that it isn't simply about being a good parent in terms of talking and listening and being there, but it's about being a good example. A dad who does not give up on himself, creates a belief in his children that they too can succeed.

You've been that kind of dad. In spite of obstacles that you could not have foreseen or events never planned, you've moved forward, embracing all that life offered and making the most out of it.

Children need that kind of example in a world that is confusing and manipulative. How will they know there are consequences to actions that can't be erased like those in a video game, if they have not seen the example in their own homes? Dad, you have shown them the way to persevere around the blind spots and the sudden

shifts in the landscape. You have made them realize that with God all things are possible.

Brother Lawrence said, "All things are possible to him who believes, yet more to him who hopes, more still to him who loves, and most of all to him who practices and perseveres in these three virtues."

You are a dad who practices and perseveres, carrying those virtues in your heart and planting them squarely in the minds of your children where they take root and grow and flourish.

Remember those early days after you first
saw the light? Those were the hard times!
Kicked around in public, targets of every
kind of abuse – some days it was you,
other days your friends. If some friends
went to prison, you stuck by them.
If some enemies broke in and seized your
goods, you let them go with a smile,
knowing they couldn't touch your
real treasure. Nothing they did
bothered you, nothing set you back.
So don't throw it all away now. You were sure
of yourselves then. It's still a sure thing!
But you need to stick it out, staying
with *God's plan* so you'll be there for
the promised completion.

- Hebrews 10:36 - THE MESSAGE-

Be of good cheer. Do not think of today's failures, but of the *success* that may come tomorrow. You have set yourselves a difficult task, but you will succeed if you persevere; and you will find *joy* in overcoming obstacles. Remember, no effort that we make to attain something beautiful is ever lost.

- Helen Keller -

Father, thank You for each day
that brings greater hope and
blessing to the work of each
dad as he strives to persevere in
bringing his children closer
to You. Be steadfast in Your
strengthening of hearts and minds
and spirits who seek to know
more of You. Bless the dad who
never sees the obstacles, but sees
Your hand at work in the lives
of his children.

Amen.

YOU ARE A GRATEFUL DAD

It's clear to others that you are a humble man, grateful for the treasures and pleasures God has given you. It's clear because no matter what life brings, you continue to believe in God's goodness and grace.

As a dad, you know the ups and downs of life and you know how hard it is to always keep the faith that things will work out the way you hope they will. You've helped instill that grateful spirit in your children as well. You've taught them that the gifts we receive from God are plentiful, but not always easy to discern; they're real, even when we can't see and touch them. Yet, in spite of those challenges, you are willing to put your heart and mind out there, grateful for whatever comes your way. You understand God's desire that we should give thanks in all circumstances. You rise each day with thanksgiving for what He puts before you.

Today, you're being thanked for giving, sharing, and tutoring the ones in your care and even in your neighborhood. When the world seems to spin out of control, you hug even tighter to the Creator, the One who holds it all in His hand, for He knows the outcome and will keep us ever in His sight. In the same way, you hold a world of gratitude in your heart and share it in a way that makes a significant difference.

Thanks for being someone who knows the secret that if you spend more time counting your blessings, you won't have much time left to count your complaints. You are being counted today among the most wonderful dads of this generation. Thanks for being a blessing to others, especially to your own children.

It is the highest and holiest of
the paradoxes that the man who
really knows he cannot pay his
debt will be forever paying it.

- G. K. Chesterton -

***

*Hallelujah!
It's a good thing to sing
praise to our God; praise is
beautiful, praise is fitting.*

- Psalm 147:1 THE MESSAGE -

Lord, thank You for shining
Your light on dads who honor You
and help others to see You more
clearly. Thank You for Your incredible
gifts and blessings that stream forth
in our lives even when we're not
able to realize them. Thank You for
giving us grateful hearts.

Amen.

THE DAD ON HIS KNEES

None of us really manage to come to our full height until we find ourselves down on our knees. As a dad, you've found plenty of opportunities to raise yourself to knee level so that you could place the care and well-being of your children in the hands of the One who can actually do something to direct their steps and keep them on the pathway. As parents, we sometimes hope we have that opportunity, and perhaps we do, but God is in control and offers the most direct route for any of us. Thanks for being a dad who knows how important it is to lavish your children in prayer.

When you're a dad who prays diligently for your children, you give them a gift beyond measure. You keep them under the wings that will both shelter them and teach them to fly. You give them a protector and guide for all that they need and desire. Since prayer is an expression of faith, it brings opportunity for connection and bonding with your children that nothing else can do. You in fact, give them a legacy of prayer and turn them into prayer warriors as well.

Martin Luther once stated that, "All who call on God in true faith, earnestly from the heart, will certainly be heard, and will receive what they have asked and desired, although not in the hour or measure, or the very thing which they ask; yet they will obtain something greater and more glorious than they had dared to ask."

A dad who dares to bring his children closer to the throne will see the outcome in ways he never dreamed possible. God not only answers, but loves to surprise the ones we love with gifts that glorify His name.

Thanks for getting on your knees every day for your children. You have raised them up in more ways than you can know. Blessings to you, Dad!

*I ask the Father in His great glory to give
you the power to be strong inwardly through
His Spirit. I pray that Christ will live in your
hearts by faith and that your life will be
strong in love and be built on love.*

- Ephesians 3:16-17 -

Lord, bless this dad with Your
gracious presence each day as he
strives to nurture his children into
strong and loving adults. Protect
the ones he loves and comfort them
in loss, fill their hearts and minds
with continual joy in knowing You.
Amen.

You're a Humble Star

Some dads are very successful in the world, but not so successful as dads or husbands. Some are good dads, but don't have any sense of purpose, so they lose their way when it comes to achieving goals in the world. Other dads are like you, successful in your own way in the world and yet able to see all that you have as gifts from God.

You don't seem to have a need to let the world think your success is all about you and that's a pretty fabulous way to be. Bless you for being a good dad and even more, a humble ambassador of the One who made you.

Much of your success comes from the attitude you have for serving others. You see yourself as called to serve your children, your family and your neighbors. That's an attitude that not only pleases everyone in your sphere of influence, but actually pleases God as well. Here are some definite ways to know that what you're doing serves God and pleases Him:

- You make it a habit to start your day with Him, creating one-on-one time for prayer and Scripture.

- You assess the motives of others by what you perceive comes from the heart.

- You lend a hand to your neighbors and offer help in any way you can.

- You set an example for your children that not only makes them proud of you, but makes them hope to be more like you.

- You work hard to shine your light at work, at home, and in any service you perform for the Lord.

- You can be sure that God loves your humble spirit and kind heart and that each day He sees you as a success in every way that matters.

Dear Lord, thank You for the generous dads with willing hearts and hands who serve their families with joy and love. Thank You for the difference they make in the world by shaping their children to be kind and loving servants as well.

Amen.

I don't know what your destiny will be, but one thing I know, the only ones among you who will be really happy are those who have sought and found how to serve.

- Albert Schweitzer -

GOOD DADS KNOW
WHEN TO LET GO!

Do you remember the last time you had to give up on something or let go of something? Maybe it was an idea that you once thought would have great impact on the world or at least on your family. Maybe it was a house you lived in, but you lost your job and had to change your direction and find a new home. Maybe it was when you sent your first child off to college and had to let go and pray for God's protection over your young adult when you couldn't be there.

Letting go isn't an easy task for any of us. Change comes with some resistance even when it is good for us. As a dad, you've witnessed many changes. You've changed in your own knowledge of parenting as the time and seasons and situations have faded into so many digital photos in the scrapbook of your life. You've changed in your awareness of what the truth is, the truth of God, of virtues and values you grew up with. You've changed, you've tried, and with some reluctance, you've learned when to let go.

There is a popular saying that states, "Let go and let God." The idea is that if we are just willing to let go of some idea, some place, some important person in our lives, God can then step in and help create the best possible scenario for that situation. We like the idea, even if we aren't good at putting it into practice. A philosopher once said, "People avoid change until the pain of remaining the same is greater than the pain of changing." There could definitely be some truth to that.

Some dads seem to think they can resist change and it will flee from them. Others seem to take it in their stride, but don't do much to proactively create positive change. Others understand that change is part of life's process and letting go of what once was is a necessary thing. Life calls all of us to have the courage to move on.

Thanks, Dad, for letting go of your children in the ways that help them grow stronger, and holding on to them in the ways that bring them joy and peace.

Let your children go if you
want to keep them.

- Malcolm Forbes -

Dear Father in heaven,

bless the dads who are facing

times of change. Those whose

heads are spinning with

wonder at all that must be done

to let go of the lives and

the children they thought they

could hold forever. Bless them

everywhere they look with

joy and courage.

Amen.

GROWING UP WITH YOUR CHILDREN

Most parents prefer to think of themselves as "grown-ups". It's a term that never seems to mean the same thing twice though, because "grown up" and being of adult stature and chronology are vastly different things. What many of us realize is how much "growing up" we do in the process of raising our children. As they learned, we learned. We might not be willing to share that with them if we think it best for them to live under the illusion that we actually had a plan for most of the house rules we placed them under. No doubt, we did the next best thing, just said a prayer and hoped things would work out somehow.

Having faith in our parenting takes a lot of time and sometimes it's not till the stage when children become adults that we can sense the amazing thing we actually did. We took a little slippery mass of wiggly skin and bones and somehow shaped it into a tiny human being, who became an amazing kid and an outstanding adult. That took some courage.

Thanks for being a remarkable dad who stepped in from the first breath your child took to the stage of releasing them into the world, and still experiences the awe and wonder of the process. Thanks for being a dad who will probably always wonder where you managed to do things right and how your child somehow managed to sidestep the errors you made and come out ahead anyway. Thanks for being a dad who knows what true grace is all about because God was certainly in the forefront of all the efforts created between you and your child.

You've been a successful parent, a loving father, and an inspiration in more ways than you may be willing to admit to your children. You've taught them the importance of balance, of faith, of laughter and hard work. You've reminded them that much of life is a mystery and that not every "Why?" has an answer. You've grown up with your children to become an amazing and effective dad.

Dear Lord, You have walked with Your sons and changed them into fathers, giving them guidance and grace and wisdom for the job. You have created a way for them to reflect Your love into the lives of those around them. Bless all dads today, Lord, granting them peace and joy in the gifts You have given them through their children.

Amen.

Behold, children are a heritage from the LORD, the fruit of the womb is a reward.

- Psalm 127:3 NKJV -

Our religion is one which **challenges** the ordinary

human standards by holding that the ideal of life

is the spirit of a little child. We tend to glorify

adulthood and wisdom and worldly prudence,

but the gospel reverses all this. The gospel says that

the inescapable condition of entrance into the divine

fellowship is that we turn and become as a

little child … God has sent children into the world,

not only to replenish it, but to serve as sacred

reminders of something ineffably **precious** which

we are always in danger of losing. The sacrament

of childhood is thus a continuing **revelation.**

– Elton Trueblood –